Only Love Will Last

D. Morgan ®

Love makes everything worthwhile

HARVEST HOUSE PUBLISHERS
Eugene, Oregon

Only Love Will Last

Text Copyright © 2000 D. Morgan
Published by Harvest House Publishers
Eugene, Oregon 97402

ISBN 0-7369-0338-0

Design and production by Koechel Peterson and Associates, Minneapolis, Minnesota

Harvest House Publishers has made every effort to trace the ownership of all poems and quotes. In the event of a question arising from the use of a poem or quote, we regret any error made and will be pleased to make the necessary correction in future editions of this book.

Scripture quotations are taken from: the Holy Bible, New International Version®, Copyright © 1973, 1978, 1984 by the International Bible Society. Used by permission of Zondervan Publishing House; and from the King James Version of the Bible.

Printed in Hong Kong

00 01 02 03 04 05 / IM / 10 9 8 7 6 5 4 3 2 1

Frame and fortune fade away…… ….Only love will last.

*My love for you
is a journey—
starting at forever
and ending at never.*

AUTHOR UNKNOWN

Love is a circle
Without ending,
Never narrow
Always bending...

—D. Morgan

What greater thing is there for two

human souls than to feel that they are joined

together to strengthen each other in all labor,

to minister to each other in all sorrow, to share with

each other in all gladness, to be one with each other

in the silent unspoken memories?

George Eliot

*True
love stories
never have endings.*

Author Unknown

My tears become rainbows...

When I Remember You.

D. Morgan

Love is a canvas furnished by Nature

Oh, inexpressible as sweet,

Love takes my voice away;

I cannot tell thee, when we meet,

What most I long to say.

But hadst thou hearing in thy heart

To know what beats in mine;

Then shouldst thou walk, where'er thou art,

In melodies divine.

G.E. WOODBERRY

nd embroidered by imagination.

VOLTAIRE

For hearing my thoughts,

understanding my dreams

and being my best friend...

For filling my life with joy

and loving me without end...

I do.

AUTHOR UNKNOWN

Our cup is full,
We've found our w

My life is for me but my

…he fruit is on the vine. Tomorrow remains a mystery…
…But today is… Yours and Mine.

…heart is for you. AUTHOR UNKNOWN

Love is a joyful gift to receive,
but far more fulfilling to give.

MAUREEN DUBOUR

I have found the one

whom my soul loves...

THE SONG OF SOLOMON

Fragile as a paper kite

Life can change

With morning light

But love endures

Forever bright

Strong as thunder...

In the night.

D. MORGAN

What would life be without a song, without a dance ~ without a little sweet romance? ~ Without a friend ~ a heart to mend? If all skies were blue above, but without love? ..... what would life be?

Life is the flower for which love

If a hug represented

how much I loved you,

I would hold you in my

arms forever.

AUTHOR UNKNOWN

s the honey.

VICTOR HUGO

March 2, 2001

On this your wedding day,

What once the

heart has owned,

No one can take away.

D. Morgan

Joanne + Simon,
Best wishes +
Love for you both
for many
years ahead.
Amy + Ali

The music plays

The heart remembers...

And the melody

Lingers

On.

D. Morgan

One hundred years together

For every day — all over again

I fall

Would surely be too few

e with you

Love

is the

greatest

refreshment

in life.

PABLO PICASSO

It is difficult to know at

what moment love begins;

it is less difficult to know

that it has begun.

HENRY WADSWORTH LONGFELLOW

Ever lovers,

Always friends,

Complete —

The circle

Never

Ends.

D. Morgan

Love makes everything worthwhile

If you would be loved, love and be lovable.

BENJAMIN FRANKLIN

So Jacob

served seven years

to get Rachel, but they seemed

like only a few days to him

because of his love for her.

The Book of Genesis

but my heart will never grow tired of loving you.

If I could reach up and hold a star for every time you've made

me smile, the entire evening sky would be in the palm of my hand.

AUTHOR UNKNOWN

If I could live forever,

And all my dreams come true ~

Here in my blue heaven.....

.....I'd spend my Life With You.

You were made perfectly to be loved ~

and surely I have loved you, the idea of you, my

ELIZABETH BARRETT BROWNING

hole life long.

Together

How happy am I, having you at my side,
Through life's ever changeable weather;
My hopes and my fears unto you I confide,
As we move heart in heart on together.

We have tasted success, we have drank of desire,
With hearts light and gay as a feather;
And the day and the deeds that our spirits inspire —
We have lived and enjoyed them together.

Through care and misfortune and trouble and pain
Made part of life's changeable weather,
And sickness and sorrow came once and again,
We met and endured them together.

So together still sharing what fate has in store,
May we go to the end of our tether;
When the good and evil things all are shared o'er,
May we share the last sleep still together.

HUNTER MACCULLOUGH

An anniversary love song is perfume from the past making memories linger in your hearts and hold you fast

Love keeps the cold out better

HENRY WADSWORTH LONGFELLOW

Love is the language
our hearts use to speak
to one another.
For you, my dear,
my heart sings.

Amanda Byrd

Come on, come on,
Let's dance
the night away —
As the world
grows colder,
And our friends
grow older...
On our Golden
Wedding
Day.

D. Morgan

han a cloak.

No, there's nothing half so sweet

THOMAS MOORE

As long as there are dreams

As long as life endures

n life as love's young dream.

Always

and forever...

t of mine is yours.

It was springtime —

Life was sweet...

And we

Were

Very

Young.

D. Morgan

Security is when I'm very much in

love with somebody extraordinary who

loves me back.

Shelley Winters

Dearest wife,

sweetheart, friend —

You are my love story...

Beginning to

End.

D. Morgan

first.... a dream.........

.... Then a plan —
Here's my heart —
Take my hand.

This is my lover, this is my friend...

The Song of Solomon

Love transcends everything.

Love, love, love, that is the

WOLFGANG AMADEUS MOZART

The most wonderful of all things in life,

I believe, is the discovery of another human

being with whom one's relationship has a glowing

depth, beauty, and joy as the years increase.

Sir Hugh Walpole

soul of genius.

Soul meets soul
on lovers' lips.

PERCY BYSSHE SHELLEY

So, fall asleep love, loved

by me...for I know love,

I am loved by thee.

Robert Browning

Thanks for the memor
With God our guid

The shoulder always there ~ the strong and tender care ~
And you beside ~ made hard times unaware.....

thank you so much

Give her

two red roses, each

with a note. The first

note says, "For the woman

I love" and the second,

"For my best friend."

AUTHOR UNKNOWN

The supreme happiness of life *is the*
conviction that we are loved.

VICTOR HUGO

whether skies are gray or blue

longer than forever Sweetheart

As long as there is sun and rain

is the

...I'll be loving you.

*L*ove in her sunny eyes does basking play;

Love walks the pleasant mazes of her hair;

Love does on both her lips forever stray;

And sows and reaps a thousand kisses there.

<small>ABRAHAM COWLEY</small>

Familiar acts are beautiful through

<small>PERCY BYSSHE SHELLEY</small>

Love is a light

that casts

a shadow

on the sun.

DONALD DANFORD

Love.

My dearest one,

Grow old with me

The best for us...

Is yet

to be.

D. Morgan

If ever two were one, then surely we.

If ever man were loved by wife, then thee;

If ever wife was happy in a man,

Compare with me ye women if you can.

I prize thy love more than whole mines of gold,

Or all the riches that the East doth hold.

ANNE BRADSTREET

Love is a circle that doth restless move
In the same sweet eternity of love.

ROBERT HERRICK

Among the dearest things I know
Are where the wild wflowers grow
Simple pleasures ~ gentle fac
Cozy little wayside places

Old love   letters tied with blue ~ the way I fe

To love and be loved is

DAVID VISCOTT

when I'm with you.

to feel the sun from both sides.

Love is not love

Which alters when it alteration finds,

Or bends with the remover to remove;

O no! It is an ever-fixed mark

That looks on tempests

and is never shaken.

WILLIAM SHAKESPEARE

Words of love are works of love.

WILLIAM R. ALGER